HO HO HO
&
HA HA HA!

500+ CHRISTMAS CRACKERS

Caroline calls her grandmother. "Oh grandma, the drum I got from you was my best Christmas gift."
"Really, my dear?" says grandmother.
"Yes, mum gives me one dollar each time I stop playing"

Where do snow-women like to dance? At snowballs.

Why does Santa Claus not like it when he gets stuck in the chimney? Because he has Claus-trophobia.

Why are Christmas trees so bad at knitting? They always drop their needles.

Paul calls his aunt: "Thank you for your Christmas present." "Oh", his aunt says. "That was nothing."
"I thought so too," Robin replies, "but mum says I have to thank you."

What happened to the man who stole an advent calendar? He got 25 days.

What is a dinosaur's least favourite reindeer? Comet.

A husband asks his wife: "What would you like for Christmas? " She replies: "I don't know."
The husband says "Alright, I'll give you another year to think about it."

1

Georgie is running through the house and yells at the top of his lungs "Dear Santa; please send me a new bicycle." His dad tells him: "Don't yell, Santa isn't deaf!" Georgie says to his dad "Santa isn't deaf, but grandma is!"

What is green and goes 'ribbit ribbit'? A Mistle-toad.

Why is Santa so good at karate? Because he's got a black belt.

What nationality is Santa? North Polish.

A lightbulb has a date with a Christmas light. He arrives at her door and knocks and is surprised to find that all of her friends will accompany them. "We're Christmas lights, she explains. When one of us goes out, we all go out!"

What is a snowman doing in the vegetable aisle? Picking his nose.

What do you call a snowman with a sunburn? A puddle!

What is white and climbs up the mountain? A homesick avalanche.

Jesus, Santa and a Turkey have a conversation together. Jesus says "You know what's annoying? When your birthday is on Christmas!" Santa says "At least you don't have to work on Christmas Eve!" Turkey says "I wish I had your problems!"

"I don't know what to get my wife for Christmas.," "Why don't you just ask her?" his friend replies. "Well, I don't want to spend that much."

A daughter says to her father: "I want a pony for Christmas." Her father replies "We always have turkey."

The two kids are fighting loud over the Christmas cookies. Their mother is completely unnerved and says "Can you two never agree on something?" The kids replied "We do! We both want the same cookie!"

Two men are talking: "I love my Christmas present, thermos flasks are a brilliant invention. During the winter it keeps the tea hot and in the summer the lemonade cold," says one man. The other man says: "How does the thermos flask know when it's winter or summer?"

Santa asks the children: "Who has been well-behaved and always did what mother asked?" The kids all say in unison: "Daddy."

After being particularly annoyed by her younger sister, the older one says: "Let's play Christmas. I'll be Santa Claus, and you can be a present, and I'll give you away."

A man is leaving church on Christmas Eve when the pastor says to the man "You need to join the Army of the Lord!" The man replies "I'm already in the Army of the Lord, Pastor." "Then how come I never see you except at Christmas and Easter?" the Pastor asks. The man whispers back, "I'm in the secret service."

What kind of money do they use at the North Pole? Cold hard cash!

You know you're starting to get old when Santa starts to look younger.

Santa asks a boy what he wants for Christmas. The boy asks for an electric train set. "If you get your train," Santa tells him, "your dad is going to want to play with it too. Is that okay?" The boy becomes very quiet. So Santa asks, "Is there anything else you would like Santa to bring you?" He promptly replied, "Another train."

I have this incredible ability to predict what's inside a wrapped present. It's a gift.

My dad gave me a Walmart gift card for Christmas. Then he said, "Don't spend it in one place."

The 3 stages of man: 1. He believes in Santa Claus. 2. He doesn't believe in Santa Claus. 3. He is Santa Claus.

Where does Santa Claus go swimming? The North Pool.

It was Christmas and the judge asked the prisoner, "What are you charged with?" "Doing my Christmas shopping early," replied the defendant. "That's no offense," said the judge. "How early were you doing this shopping?" "Before the store opened."

What did the gingerbread man put on his bed? A cookie sheet.

"I want a dog for Christmas", Sophie says. "I've been a good girl, I always eat my veggies, clean my room and do my homework." Her mother shakes her head: "I know dear, but wish for something else." Sophie thinks about it, then she says "Okay, I wish to swap roles with you for one whole day." Her mother agrees. Sophie smiles and goes to grab her coat. "Alright, then let's go to the city now to buy Sophie a dog."

What did octopus get for Christmas? 4 pairs of socks!

Peter asks for a trumpet for Christmas, but his dad won't have it and says "I don't want to listen to this noise all day." "But Dad," says Peter, "I promise you, I will only play when you're asleep."

How does Christmas Eve end? With an "E".

What is a monkey's favourite Christmas song? "Jungle Bells".

Why do snowmen never pay their bills? Because all of their accounts are frozen.

A little boy asks Santa: "Do you also have to wash your face or just comb it?"

Knock knock. Who's there? Scold. Scold who? Scold outside, let me in!

Which hand is it better to write your Christmas list with? Neither, it's better to write with a pencil!

What did one snowman say to the other snowman? It smells like carrots over here!

Spencer: What are you giving your little brother for Christmas? Johnny: I haven't decided yet. Spencer: What did you give him last year? Johnny: Measles.

The mother says to her son: "Please light up the Christmas tree." After some time, he returns and asks: "The candles too?

How can we be so sure Santa Claus is a man? Simple! A woman would never wear the same dress every year.

At a monastery the monks have a vow of silence. Only at Christmas, and only by one monk, and only with one sentence, is the vow allowed to be broken. One Christmas, Brother Thomas says, "I like the mashed potatoes we have with the Christmas turkey!" and he sits down. Silence ensues for 365 days. The next Christmas, Brother Michael gets his turn, and he says "I think the mashed potatoes are lumpy and I hate them!" Once again, silence for one year. The following Christmas, Brother Paul rises and says, "I'm fed up with this constant bickering!"

What sort of ball doesn't bounce? A snowball!

What do you get if you cross an apple with a Christmas tree? A pine-apple!

What do you give a train driver for Christmas? Platform shoes!

Santa Claus was sitting in the mall waiting for children to tell him their wishes when a young lady about twenty years old walked up and sat on his lap. Santa doesn't usually take requests from adults, but she smiled very nicely at him, so he asked her, "What do you want for Christmas?" "Something for my mother, please", said the young lady. "Something for your mother? Well, that's very thoughtful of you," smiled Santa. "What do you want me to bring her?"

Without hesitation, she replied, "A son-in-law!"

What's the best thing to put into a Christmas cake? Your teeth!

Why couldn't the butterfly go to the Christmas dance? It was a moth ball!

Teacher: If you had $1 and you asked Mr. Scrooge for another, how many dollars would you have? Student: One. Teacher: You don't know your Maths. Student: You don't know Mr. Scrooge.

Who is Santa's least favorite reindeer? Rude-olph.

A man was driving down the road when a policeman stopped him. The officer looked in the back of the man's truck and said, "Why is there a reindeer in your truck?" "That is my reindeer", the man replied. "It belongs to me." "You need to take it to the zoo," the policeman said. The next day, the officer saw the same guy driving down the road. He pulled him over again. He saw the reindeer was still in the truck, but it was wearing water wings this time. "I thought I told you to take this reindeer to the zoo!" the officer said. "I did," the man replied. "And today I'm taking it to the pool."

What did one candy cane say to the other? We're mint for each other!

Cross a bell and a skunk and get Jingle smells.

A father opens a Christmas card he got from his son. It reads: "Merry Christmas, Dad. Don't worry about the past – you can't change it. Don't worry about the future – you can't predict it. And don't worry about the present – I didn't get you one."

Why couldn't the skeleton go to the Christmas Party? He had no body to go with.

What do snowmen eat for breakfast? Frosted Flakes!

Marcus's mom: "Marcus, there were two pieces of Christmas cake in the kitchen, and now there's only one. Can you explain that?" Marcus: "I guess I didn't see the other piece."

Bobby's trying to earn some money for Christmas presents. He goes around his neighbourhood looking for a job. One neighbour offers him some money to paint his porch. Bobby agrees and goes to work. A few hours later, he knocks on the neighbour's door and says, "I'm all finished, but you should know that your car is a Mercedes."

One snowman to the other: "What's orange and sounds like a parrot?" "A carrot."

Why don't snowmen like carrot cake? - Because it tastes like boogers.

Who delivers presents to cats? Santa Claws!

Why didn't the crab make any Christmas presents? Because he was shellfish!

Whydidn't the teddy bear eat his dessert at Christmas dinner? Because he was stuffed!

What falls at the North Pole but never gets hurt? Snow!

When does a reindeer have a trunk? When it goes on vacation.

Why is Santa so jolly? He knows where all the toys are!

A young woman visits her husband's grandpa with him for the holidays. Everything is beautifully decorated, and the grandfather is charming to her, but while having lunch, the young woman notices something on her plate. "Are these plates clean?" she asks. The grandpa replies, "They're as clean as cold water can get them. Just go ahead and finish your meal." At dinner, the woman inspected the plates and again was concerned, she could see some of the leftover egg from that morning on them. "Are you sure these plates are clean?" she asks. Grandpa says, "I told you before, those dishes are as clean as cold water can get them!" Later, as she and her husband are leaving, the grandpa's dog starts to growl and doesn't let them pass. The young woman says: "Your dog won't let me get out!" Grandpa turns to the dog and yells, "Cold Water, go lie down!"

When does Christmas come before Thanksgiving? In the dictionary!

What's red, white, and blue at Christmas dinner? A sad candy cane!

What's a parent's favourite Christmas carol? Silent Night!

Why are Christmas trees so fond of the past? Because the present's beneath them.

What does Jack Frost like about school? Snow and tell.

Where do polar bears vote? The North Poll!

What do elves do after school? Their gnome work!

The teacher asks her student: "If you eat half of a Christmas pudding and your sister eats the other half, what are you left with?" Student: "Angry parents."

What can you catch in the winter with your eyes closed? A cold!

What do snowmen call their kids? Chill-dren!

What's the difference between Santa's reindeer and a knight? One slays the dragon, and the other's draggin the sleigh.

When asked about his job, Frosty always replies, "There's no business like snow business."

What is a Christmas tree's favourite candy? Ornamints.

Mum: Santa can't come if your room looks like that. Go pick it up. Emma: I can't. Mum: Why not? Emma: It's too heavy.

Why was Santa's little helper depressed? Because he had low elf esteem!

What does Santa say at the start of a race? "Ready, set, Ho! Ho! Ho!"

What does a stormcloud get for Christmas? Thunderwear!

On Christmas Eve, the son turns to his father: "Dad, can you turn the heat up? I am freezing." The dad replies: "Go to the corner it's 90 degrees."

What does a painter do when it snows? He puts on another coat.

A rooster and an elephant decided to go on a trip for Christmas. Who takes less time to pack his things? The rooster – he only takes a comb, the elephant takes his whole trunk!

What do road crews use at the North Pole? Snow cones!

What did the plate say to the fork at the Christmas Dinner? "Dinner is on me."

Why don't dinosaurs celebrate Christmas? Because they are extinct.

Bob went to visit his friend Tom, and because it was right after Christmas, he decided to give him a chessboard as a present. They played two games, then Bob had to take a phone call and was gone for some time. When he returned to the room, he was amazed to find that the dog had taken his seat and was playing with Tom. Bob watched the game for a while. "I can hardly believe my eyes!" he said. "That's the smartest dog I've ever seen." "He's not so smart," Tom replied. "I've won the last two games."

What do you call a canine in winter? A Chilidog.

Mrs Peters went to a pet shop because she wanted to surprise her family with a dog for Christmas. "May I please have that husky for my son?" she asked the cashier. "Sorry," the cashier replied. "We don't trade."

What animal wears a coat all winter and pants in the summer? A dog.

What happens to ice when it gets mad? It has a meltdown.

What did one ice cube say to the other? "I'm cooler than you!"

A woman was picking through the frozen turkeys at the grocery store but couldn't find one big enough for her family. She asked an employee, "Do these turkeys get any bigger?" "No, they're dead."

Why did the cranberries turn red? Because they saw the turkey dressing!

What do elves like to listen to? Wrap music.

What do skeleton's get for Christmas? A xylabone.

A man is staying in a hotel for a Christmas vacation. He walks up to the front desk and says, "Sorry. I forgot what room I'm in." The receptionist replies, "No problem, this is the lobby."

If Santa drops his red hat into the blue sea, what does it become? Wet.

On which side of the house do pine trees grow? The outside.

How do you make a milkshake? You put a cow on the north pole.

Why don't kangaroos celebrate Christmas? They can't fit the tree into their pouch.

What's the dress code for a knife's Christmas party? There is none, just dress sharp.

A grandmother sat on her porch knitting three socks when someone walked by and asked, "Why are you knitting three socks?" The grandmother replied, "Because my grandson said he'd grown a foot since joining the Army."

How do aliens wrap their Christmas gifts? They use astro-knots.

What do you call a turkey after Thanksgiving? Lucky.

What did the Christmas tree say when it couldn't figure out the math problem? "I'm stumped."

Why can't the skunk afford any Christmas presents? Because he only has one scent.

A little boy gives his father a package of gum for Christmas. The father looks a little confused, but the boy explains: "It doesn't look like much, but it's mint." "Did you hear about the Christmas party on the moon?" "No, how was it?" "It had great food, but no atmosphere."

What does a mountain wear in the cold? An ice cap.

I was going to tell you this joke about a Christmas party with really good refreshments. I can't remember the entire joke. But I know there was a long punch line.

Santa and one of his reindeer walk into a movie theater. "I'm afraid I can't let your reindeer in sir," the manager says. "Oh, I assure you, he's very well behaved," Santa says. "All right then," the manager says. "If you're sure. ..." After the movie, the manager approaches Santa and says, "I'm very surprised! Your reindeer was well behaved, and even seemed to enjoy the movie!" "Yes, I was surprised, too," says Santa. "He hated the book."

Why do mummies like the holidays so much? They're into all the wrapping.

Why did the ghost sing off key at the Christmas concert? It left its sheet music at home.

What kind of guitar always has a cold? An achoo-stic!

How did the astronauts organize their Christmas party? They planet!

How did the ocean greet Santa? It waved.

What do you get when you cross a turkey with an octopus? Drumsticks for everyone at Christmas.

What did the pepper say? Season's greetings.

Which animal writes the best holiday cards? A pen-guin.

She: What would you like for Christmas? He: I want something that goes from 1 to 100 in four seconds. She: Alright, I'll get you a scale.

Don't invite the pig to the Christmas party, he's a boar!

Why do Dasher and Dancer love coffee? Because they're Santa's star bucks!

Why did Rudolph get a bad report card? Because he went down in history.

Why did the robot go on Christmas vacation? He needed to recharge his batteries.

What do you call a shark that brings presents on Christmas? Santa Jaws!

What does a grumpy sheep say at Christmas? "Baaaa humbug!"

What kind of shoes did the mice get for Christmas? Squeakers.

Where do cows buy Christmas presents? A cattle-og.

What do skeletons say before Christmas dinner? Bone appetite.

What did the skunk get for Christmas? A best-smeller!

I think I'll wear only one boot today. I heard there's only a 50 percent chance of snow.

What do snowmen like to do on the weekend? Chill out.

Why should you invite the electrical outlets to your Christmas party? Because they can always spark a conversation.

Mary: My grandmother came to visit us or Christmas vacation. Teacher: How nice! Did you meet her at the airport? Mary: Oh, no. I've known her for years!

It is Christmas, even in Gotham, and Alfred and Batman exchange gifts. Batman carefully unwraps his present. It is a new utility belt. He tries to put it on, but it just doesn't fit, he is too big. Alfred turns his head and exclaims "What a waist!"

20

What's the worst place to get your dog a Christmas present from? The flea market.

What did the turkey say to the computer? "Google, google, google."

What key has legs and can't open doors? A turkey.

The sister says to her brother: "Mum wants you to help us fix Christmas dinner."

The brother replies: "Why? Is it broken?"
What do you call a penguin at the north pole? Lost.

If H_2O is the formula for water, what's the formula for ice? H_2O cubed.

What do fish sing during winter? Christmas corals.

A man stares out of the window: "Look at this! It's supposed to snow on Christmas, not be this beastly weather we're having!", he complains. His wife looks over his shoulder and asks "What do you mean?" "It's raining cats and dogs!"

Why couldn't the beluga make it to Christmas dinner? It didn't feel too whale.

What kind of motorcycle does Santa ride? A "Holly" Davidson.

What place is never icy? A beach, because it's always sanded.

Why did the man sit on a clock at Christmas eve? Because he was told to work overtime.

Why didn't the airplane get any Christmas presents? Because of its bad altitude.

The grandmother has arrived to bring her grandchildren their Christmas presents. They unwrap them excitedly and find some cozy sweaters inside. "Did you know it takes three sheep to make one sweater?" the grandmother asks. Her grandchild replies "I didn't even know they could knit!"

Why does Santa go through the chimney? Because it soots him.

What is a bird's favourite Christmas story? The Finch Who Stole Christmas.

What does Christmas have to do with a cat lost in the desert? They both have sandy claws.

What do male cattle use to write their Christmas wish list? Bullpens!

What's the difference between the Christmas alphabet and the ordinary alphabet? The Christmas alphabet has Noel.

Wha do you call a child that doesn't believe in Santa? A rebel without a Claus.

Why did Santa go to a psychiatrist? He didn't believe in himself.

Where does Santa takes his reindeers when their tails fall off? To the retail store.

What is a child's favourite Christmas king? The stocking.

What body part do you only see during Christmas? Mistletoe.

How does the elf get to Santa's workshop? By icicle.

Knock, knock. Who's there? Lettuce. Lettuce who? Lettuce in, it's cold out here!

What does Santa bring naughty boys and girls on Christmas Eve? A pack of batteries with a note saying "toy not included".

It was a very cold winter a grandmother decided to buy Cindy a pair of earmuffs. As it was getting colder and colder, she saw however that Cindy wasn't wearing them, not even on the coldest snowy day, so she finally asked: "Didn't you like the earmuffs?" "They are beautiful", Cindy replied. "Then why don't you wear them?" the grandmother asked. Cindy said, "I was wearing them, and mum offered me some candy, but I didn't hear her! I'll never wear them again!"

How do sheep in Mexico say Merry Christmas? Fleece Navidad.

Why can't you trust baked food during the holidays? It might be a minced spy.

What do you call an elf wearing ear muffs? Anything you want. He can't hear you.

What goes "oh oh oh"? Santa walking backwards.

What do you call the wrapping paper leftover from opening presents? A Christ-mess.

Who delivers Christmas presents to dogs? Santa paws! And who delivers Christmas presents to cats? Santa claws!

What cars do elfs drive? A toy yota.

An elderly couple goes to church for the Christmas service. Halfway through, the wife leans over and whispers in her husband's ear, "I've just let out a silent fart. What do you think I should do?" The husband replies, "Put a new battery in your hearing aid."

What do you learn at Santa's Helpers school? The elf-a-bet.

What do you call a can that has the Christmas spirit? A Merry can.

Where does Santa and his reindeer go to get hot chocolate? Star-bucks.

What do reindeer hang on their Christmas trees? Horn-Aments.

What show does a squirrel see on Christmas Day? The Nutcracker.

What do you call a snowman on rollerblades? A snowmobile.

Thomas helps his mother put up the Christmas decoration. "What are we celebrating this Christmas?", he asks. His mother replies: "The birth of Jesus." "Wasn't he born last year?"

Where does Santa stay when he is on vacation? A Ho-Ho-Ho-Tel.

A little girl went to see Santa in the mall. As she climbed onto his lap, Santa asked her "And what would you like for Christmas?" The girl stared at him open-mouthed and confused for a minute, then gasped, "Didn't you get my E-mail?"

Why did the eggnog go to school? To get egg-u-cated.

What's an ig? A snow house without a loo!

What do snowmen eat for lunch? Icebergers.

What do you call Santa at the South Pole? A lost clause.

A man asks his friend: "How do you always get exactly what you wish for Christmas?" "That's easy", he replies, "A week before Christmas I start talking in my sleep."

How do you know if there's a snowman in your bed? You wake up wet.

Why does Scrooge love all of the reindeer? Because every buck is dear to him!

Did you hear about the time Scrooge pretended to be Santa Claus? He slid down chimneys and asked, "Who wants to buy a toy?"

When are your eyes not eyes? When the cold wind makes them water!

If you live in an igloo, what's the worst thing about global warming? No privacy.

Why did Marty take a prune to the Christmas party? Because he couldn't find a date.

What do you get when you cross a snowman with a radio? Cool Music.

What do you call a frozen dog? A pupsicle.

"Tommy", the mum asks, "do you know where I put the box of Christmas cookies? "Yes", Tommy replies. "It's up in the cupboard behind …" "Ah, alright", his mum interrupts. "I'll find a new place."

After the Christmas dinner, Danny turns to his mum. "Mum, can I get two pieces of Chocolate cake for dessert?" "Of course, honey. Just let me cut your piece in half."

How does Christmas end? With an "S".

How can you get a stupid person to laugh on New Years? You tell them a joke on Christmas eve.

Santa is trying to explain the concept of Christmas to a polar bear. The bear looks confused however, scratches his head and finally says: "I barely understand."

How did the ornament get addicted to Christmas? He was hooked on trees his whole life.

How much did Santa pay for his sleigh? Nothing. It was on the house!

What did Adam say to his wife on Christmas? It's finally Christmas, Eve!

What do you call Santa on a break? Santa Pause.

Where does mistletoe go to get famous? Holly-wood!

A snowman says to the other: "I have gained so much weight over Christmas! What do you do to lose weight?" The other replies: "Just wait for the weather to get warmer."

What is the popular carol in the desert? Camel ye Faithful.

Why can't the Christmas tree stand up? It doesn't have legs.

What's a good Christmas tip? Never catch snowflakes with your tongue until all the birds have gone south for the winter.

What did one candle say to the other on Christmas Eve? I am going out for dinner tonight.

Why did the kids start eating the puzzle on Christmas? Because their father said that it was a piece of cake!

A man bought his wife beautiful diamond earrings for Christmas. After hearing about this extravagant gift, a friend of his said, "I thought she wanted one of those sporty four-wheel-drive vehicles." "She did," he replied. "But where was I going to find a fake Jeep?"

What's a snowman's favorite Mexican food? Brrrrrr-itos!

How do cats greet each other at Christmas? "A Furry Christmas & Happy mew year!"

How one snowman greets the other one? Ice to meet you.

What do you call an elf that just won the lottery? Welfy.

How does Rudolph know when Christmas is coming? He looks at his calen-deer!

Why did the elves ask the turkey to join their band? Because he had the drum sticks!

How do you scare a snowman? Get a hairdryer!

What sort of cakes do snowmen like? Any kind, as long as it has thick icing!

A woman lost her handbag while Christmas shopping. An honest little boy found it and returned it to her. Looking in her purse, she commented, "Hmmm... That's odd. When I lost my bag, there was a $20 bill in it. Now there are twenty $1 bills." The boy quickly replied, "That's right. The last time I found a lady's purse, she didn't have any change for a reward."

What type of pine has the sharpest needles? A porcupine.

How long should an elf's legs be? Just long enough to reach the ground!

The reindeers are watching Santa clean up his workshop after Christmas. "He seems so sad", one of them says. "Don't worry about it", another one states, "it happens every year. He just gets a little Santamental."

What beats his chest and swings from Christmas cake to Christmas cake? Tarzipan!

What do vampires put on Christmas dinner? Grave-y!

How can you recognize a stupid turkey? It's looking forward to Christmas!

What did the vegetables say at the Christmas party? "Lettuce turnip the beet."

What did the big angel say to the little angel on Christmas Eve? Halo there!

A guy is sitting on a plane next to a beautiful girl. Looking for an excuse to talk to her, he turns to her and says "Wow your perfume smells amazing! Could you please tell me what brand it is so that I can buy it for my sister?" The woman turns to him and says "Oh, I wouldn't do that if I were you. Some idiot might find an excuse to talk to her!"

What do you get if you cross Christmas with a detective? Santa Clues!

What's brown, tasty and sneaks around the kitchen? Mince spies.

What does December have that no other month has? The letter "D".

How can Santa deliver presents during a thunderstorm? His sleigh is flown by rain-deer.

What's red and white and falls down the chimney? Santa Klutz!

What did the peanut butter say to the grape on Christmas? "'Tis the season to be jelly!"

What do you call an elf who steals gift wrapping from the rich to give to the poor? Ribbon Hood.

Where do you find reindeer? It depends on where you leave them!

What do reindeer say before they tell a joke? This will sleigh you.

What is Santa's primary language? North Polish.

How can you tell that a family doesn't celebrate Christmas? The lights are on, but nobody's a gnome.

What do you call a bankrupt Santa? Saint Nickel-less.

Why did the apple cross the road on Christmas eve? To get to Granny Smith's house!

A man was looking for a Christmas gift for his wife. Always short of money, he thought about what that present might be, but couldn't come up with anything. So he entered the cosmetics section of a store and asked the salesgirl. She brought him to the perfume register and showed him a bottle $75. "Too expensive," he replied. The young lady returned with a smaller bottle for $50. "Oh dear," he exclaimed, "still far too much." Growing annoyed at his behaviour, the salesgirl brought out a tiny $10 bottle and offered it to him. He became agitated, "What I mean", he whined, "is I'd like to see something dirt cheap." So the sales girl handed him a mirror.

What did the stamp say to the Christmas card? Stick with me, and we'll go places!

Why don't you ever see Santa in the hospital? Because he has private elf care!

How did Scrooge win the football game? The ghost of Christmas passed!

What do angry mice send to each other at Christmas? Cross-mouse cards!

What did Santa say to the smoker? Please don't smoke; it's bad for my elf!

What goes Ho Ho Whoosh, Ho Ho Whoosh? Santa going through a revolving door!

What happened to the turkey at Christmas? It got gobbled!

How does Darth Vader enjoy his Christmas Turkey? On the dark side!

Why did Santa get a parking ticket on Christmas Eve? He left his sleigh in a snow parking zone!

What do the elves cook with? Utinsels!

What is the most competitive season? Win-ter!

Why wouldn't the cat climb the Christmas tree? It was afraid of the bark.

What type of key do you need for a Nativity play? A don-key!

Anna was looking forward to the Christmas office party but needed a new dress for it. In the clothing store, she asked, "May I try on that dress in the window, please?" "Certainly not, madam," responded the salesgirl, "You'll have to use the fitting room like everyone else."

A man complains to his wife about Christmas dinner. "This turkey tastes like an old sofa..." She replies "Well I thought you liked stuffing."

What do you call a blind reindeer? I have no eye deer.

What can you sense when Santa's around? His resents.

Why did the Grinch go to the liquor store? He was searching for some holiday spirit.

What do you call Santa on a break? Santa Pause.

What is an elf's favorite sport? North-pole vaulting.

Why was the little boy so cold on Christmas morning? Because it was Decembrrrrr!

36

How do chickens dance at a holiday party? Chick to chick.

What do snowmen take when it gets too hot? A chill pill.

What falls in winter, but never gets hurt? Snow!

Why did the cookie go to the hospital? Because he felt crummy.

What did the volcano say when he saw Santa fly over him? I lava you!

What game did the tornado get for Christmas? Twister!

Although Kevin and his family had an artificial tree at home, he wanted to let his children participate in the picking of a Christmas tree. So he asked his parents if they could join them. It was great fun for everybody, so when he announced the next year that they would help the grandparents to pick a tree, he expected his six-year-old to be excited. Instead, he looked puzzled and asked: "What did they do with the one we got them last year?"

Why couldn't the pony go for Christmas carolling? It was a little horse.

How did the cat bake the Christmas cake? From scratch.

What's a Christmas bread rom-com? Loaf Actually!

What's the Grinch's least favourite band? The Who!

Where do you keep a Christmas tree? Between a Christmas two and a Christmas four.

A man comes to the doctor and says: "I've got some mince pie stuck up in my nose." The doctor takes a look at it, then nods solemnly and says "What you need is some cream."

Why do snowmen like living at the North Pole? It's cool.

What is red, white and green? A sick Santa.

What happened when the snowgirl fought with the snowboy? She gave him the cold shoulder.

A wife was excited to find lots of Christmas presents underneath the tree. She started to unwrap them and found books in all of them. Her husband looked over her shoulder and said: "Please don't forget, they have to be back in the library within two weeks."

What's red and white, red and white, red and white? Santa rolling down a hill!

Santa has three gardens so he can hoe, hoe, hoe!

What does Frosty's wife put on her face at night? Cold cream!

What's the difference between someone who doesn't understand figures of speech and the Grinch? The first takes things literally. The other takes things, literally!

So far, Humpty Dumpty is having a terrible winter. It's a shame because he had such a great fall!

What did the tree say after a long winter "What a re-leaf!"

What did the snowman say to the annoying carrot? Get out of my face!

A book never written: "What Did I Do Wrong THIS Year?" by Kole N. Stocking

What do robots wear in the winter? Roboots!

Did you hear about the guy that got hit by a snowball? It knocked him out cold!

Malcom and Brian were fortunate enough to have a season ticket for their favourite football club. Whenever they went there, however, they noticed a spare seat next right next to them. They had a friend who would love to buy a season ticket, especially if all three could have seats together, so during one half-time Malcom went to the ticket office and asked if they could buy the season ticket for this seat. The official said that unfortunately the ticket had been sold. Nevertheless, week after week, the seat was still empty. Then on Boxing day, much to Malcom and Brian's amazement the seat was taken for the first time that season. Brian couldn't resist asking the newcomer where he had been all season. "Don't ask" he said, "my wife bought the season ticket back last summer and kept it as a surprise Christmas present".

Why does it take longer to build a stupid snowman? You have to hollow out its head first.

What is Father Christmas' wife called? Mary Christmas.

Why shouldn't you invite drills for your Christmas party? Because they're boring.

Claire went shopping at a toy store when she saw a que in front of the doll counter. It was filled with people waiting for the shelves to be restocked with Mattel dolls. She realised that one of the people waiting was a good friend of hers. She knew that he did not have any children or nieces of his own, so she wondered why he was looking to buy a doll for Christmas. "I didn't realise you collected dolls", she said as she approached him. "I don't", he replied, "I've just never been able to resist a Barbie queue."

How can you recognize a stupid turkey? He's looking forward to Christmas.

What happened when the Grinch went to the flea circus? He stole the show!

A wife is annoyed by her husband. "Each year for 25 years I gave you striped socks for Christmas and now suddenly this year don't want them anymore?"

Peter thinks about the Christmas of his youth. "Now I know why Christmas was better back then... I didn't have to pay for the presents."

How do the elves clean Santa's sleigh on the day after Christmas? They use Santa-tizer.

What did the wise men say after they offered up their gifts of gold and frankincense? Wait, there's myrrh.

Children who don't learn to tie their shoes properly are bound to wind up on the knotty list.

What should you do if your car stalls on Christmas Eve? You get a mistletow.

How fast did the Grinch's sleigh go? Max speed!

What was Santa's favorite subject in school? Chemistree.

A young man driving his car got lost in a snowstorm. He didn't panic because he remembered what his dad had once told him. "If you ever get stuck in a snowstorm, just wait for a snowplough to come by and follow it." Sure enough, pretty soon a snowplough came by, and so he started to follow it. He followed it for about forty-five minutes. Finally the driver of the truck got out and asked him what he was doing. The young man explained that his dad had told him if he ever got stuck in a snowstorm, to follow a plow. The driver nodded and said, "Well, I'm done with the Wal-Mart parking lot, do you want to follow me over to Best Buy now?"

Why are Mary and Joseph role models for couples?
Because they had a stable relationship.

How did Harry Potter know what he was getting for
Christmas? He was fluent in Parceltongue.

Why did Rudolph have the complete works of
Shakespeare on his top lip?
Because his nose was well red.

What operating system do Advent calendars use?
Windows 24.

How do you keep a turkey in suspense? I will tell you
tomorrow.

Why won't the two rappers be having turkey together
this year? Because they have beef with each other.

A man watches excited as his wife opens her Christmas
present in front of him. To both their surprise it
contains a lot of leaves and vines. He cries: "That's
the last time I order from Amazon."

Will Father Christmas launch an online alternative to his
usual delivery service? He's toying with the idea.

What do recovering chocoholics have during Christmas? Cold turkey.

What is Father Christmas's favourite TV programme? The Xmas Factor.

In what year does New Year's Day come before Christmas? Every year!

What do you call a picture with an elf in it? An elfie.

How does a frog open his Christmas present? Rippit! Rippit! Rippit!

What did the gingerbread man get when he broke his leg? A candy cane.

How do chickens send Christmas cards? In henvelopes.

Justbefore Xmas, an honest politician, a generous lawyer and Santa Claus all got into the lift of a hotel. As the lift travelled from the 3rd floor down to the ground level, one-by-one they noticed a $50 note lying on the lift's floor. Which one picked up the $50 note, and handed it in at reception? Santa of course, the other two don't actually exist!

Why did the reindeer wear sunglasses to the Christmas party? Because he didn't want to be recognised!

Two women try to decorate the house at Christmas time. They struggle with the lights and are not sure if they're working. So they agree that one of them will go outside to check. The other one stays inside, turns the lights on and asks: "Are they on?" Back comes the yell of the other one: "Yes, no, yes, no, yes, no."

Why doesn't Santa let his elves work on his computer? Because they delete all of his Christmas cookies.

How does Santa measure his way? With Santa-meters.

A book never written: "How to Decorate a Tree" by Orna Ment.

Why should Christmas dinner always be well done? So you can say "Merry Crispness"!

"Do you ever buy any Christmas Seals?" "No, I wouldn't know how to feed them."

What kind of bread do elves make sandwiches with? Shortbread of course!

When should you give reindeer milk to a baby? When it's a baby reindeer!

An English man and an Irish man are driving head-on, on the night before Christmas down a twisty, dark road. Both are driving too fast for the conditions and collide on a sharp bend in the road. To the amazement of both, they are unscathed, though their cars are both destroyed. In celebration of their luck and the upcoming Christmas, both agree to put aside their dislike for the other from that moment on. At this point, the Englishman goes to the boot and fetches a 12-year-old bottle of whiskey. He hands the bottle to the Irish man, who exclaims "May the Irish and the English live together forever, in peace and harmony." The Irish man then gulps half of the bottle down. As he goes to hand the bottle to the Englishman, he replies "No thanks, I'll just wait till the police get here."

How do elves greet each other? "Small world, isn't it?"

Why does Santa have a white beard? So he can hide at the North Pole!

What does Santa use when fishing? His north pole!

What is twenty feet tall, has sharp teeth and goes Ho Ho Ho? Tyranno-santa Rex!

How do we know Santa is such a good race car driver? Because he's always in pole position!

How many elves does it take to change a lightbulb? Ten. One to change the bulb and nine to stand on each other's shoulders!

Who are Frosty's parents? Mom and Pop-Sicle!

What's the difference between Batman and the Grinch? Batman can go into Whoville without Robin.

Why is the turkey such a fashionable bird? Because he's always well dressed when he comes to dinner!

What did the Grinch get for Christmas? Mean-opoly!

Santa rides in a sleigh. What do elves ride in? Minivans!

What did the car say to the dreidel? Want to go for a spin?

Knock Knock. Who's there? Mary. Mary who? Mary Christmas!

How do Chihuahua's say Merry Christmas? Fleas Navidog!

Why did the gingerbread man go to the doctor? Because he was feeling crummy!

Why has Santa been banned from sooty chimneys? Because of his carbon footprints.

I got a Christmas card full of rice in the post today. I think it was from my Uncle Ben.

"What are you getting your wife for Christmas?", one friend asked the other. "I asked her what she wanted", the other replied. "And she said 'Get me something with diamonds'. So I'm giving her a pack of playing cards."

Why do reindeer wear fur coats? Because they look silly in snowsuits!

Who is Frosty's favourite Aunt? Aunt Artica!

Why is Parliament like ancient Bethlehem? It takes a miracle to find three wise men there.

Why was the Grinch such a great gardener? He has a green thumb.

What's faster: hot or cold? Hot, because everyone catches a cold.

How does the snow globe feel this year? A little shaken!

What do clams do for Christmas? They shellabrate.

Michael's mum stood in front of the candles. "I think the red candle burns longer than the white one", she said. Michael joined her, gave the candles one look and replied: "No, they both burn shorter."

A husband reels off a list of presents he suggests buying his wife for Christmas. "What would you like, Monica? A Jaguar? A sable coat? A diamond necklace?" "Rupert," she says. "I want a divorce". "My goodness," he says. "I wasn't planning on spending that much."

A book never written: "The Art of Giving" by Phil Anthropy.

A woman calls her friend to wish her Merry Christmas. To give it a different spin this year, she decides to sing "We wish you a Merry Christmas" to her over the phone. Half-way through she realises she's rung the wrong number. "Why didn't you stop me when you realise it was a wrong number," she asks the lady on the other end of the phone. "My dear, you need all the practice you can get!"

Why was the Christmas cake as hard as a rock? Because it was marble cake!

Every year on Christmas, Debbie looked forward to her aunt's gift—a scarf, hat, or sweater knitted by hand. One year, she must have had better things to do because Debbie received a ball of yarn, knitting needles, and a how-to-knit book. Her card read "Scarf, some assembly required."

Why did the girl put the cookies in the freezer? She wanted to ice them.

What did the elephant want for Christmas? A trunk full of gifts.

Why couldn't prehistoric man send Christmas cards? The stamps kept falling off the rocks!

What did one candle say to the other? Christmas always burns me up.

What do you give nine-hundred-pound gorilla for Christmas? I don't know, but I hope he likes it!

What's a basketball player's favourite Christmas snack? Cookies, because they can dunk them.

A man asked his girlfriend what she would like for Christmas. She said: "Well, I dreamt of a golden ring with lots of small diamonds." He asked her: "What do you think it means?" She smiled and said: "I don't know..." Two weeks later on Christmas, all the family members gathered to exchange presents. Barely containing her excitement, the girlfriend opened her present to find a book called 'Dreams and their Meanings'.

What's the name of the Lord that gives the best presents? Sir Prize!

If you don't know what to give your friends as a Christmas present, just give them a fridge, and watch their face light up as they open it.

Why did Sue's parents hide her Christmas gifts?
Because they wanted her to be Sue-prised!

The best thing about opening presents signed by "mom and dad" is the fact that my dad is just as surprised about what's in there as I am.

What kind of medal would Santa Claus win? A Noel Prize.

My friend got me a telekinetic abacus for my birthday. It wasn't my favorite present, but it's the thought that counts.

Noah is sitting at the kitchen table and looks a little pale in his face. His dad enters the room and asks him what's wrong. "I ate too much raw cookie dough and now I feel sick", he replies. His dad looks at him, measures his temperature and nods finally. "Looks like an overdoughse."

What did the injured elf get as a late Christmas present? New ears.

What does Santa like for breakfast?Mistle-"toast"!

I hate wrapping presents. They sound horrible!

Why did 25 letters of the alphabet get coal for Christmas? Because they were not E.

Thomas has never been to his friend Rebecca's place. This year, however, she invited him for Christmas. "What's the best way to find your apartment?" he asks. "Oh, it's really easy. When you reach my street, you'll see the great big tower-block. You will need to be buzzed in, so dial our number with your nose and we'll let you in. Once, you're in the building, press the button for the elevator with your elbow. Then select floor number 5 with your elbow. Our door is on the left-hand side. Knock at the door with your forehead and I'll let you in." "Ok, I got it", he replies. "But, I wonder, why can't I do all of this with my hands?" "Well, I hope you'll be bringing some presents of course."

Two friends meet. "My wife said if I bought her one more stupid present, she would burn it", the one says. "So what did you do?" the other replied. "I bought her a candle."

What is a snow shaped batman made of? Just-ice.

Why doesn't the Grinch like knock-knock jokes? Because there's always Whos there!

Carl asks his boss, "Can I get two weeks of vacation during Christmas?" His boss replies "It's May." Carl nods and says "I'm sorry. May I get two weeks off during Christmas?"

Steven was at a Christmas party with a beautiful German girl. He noticed that she was standing directly underneath a Mistletoe. As he approached her, he asked flirtatiously "Oh, what's that little thing above you?" "Its called an umlaut."

A man called his son that lived on the other end of the country the day before Christmas Eve: "I hate to ruin your day but I have to tell you that your other and I are divorcing." "Dad, what are you talking about?" the son replied shocked. "We can't stand the sight of each other any longer" the father said. "We're sick of each other and I'm sick of talking about this, so you call your sister and tell her." Frantically, the son calls his sister, who is just as shocked as he is. "Don't worry", she said, "I'll take care of this!" Immediately she called her parents and said "You are NOT getting divorced. Don't do a single thing until I get there. I'm calling my brother back, and we'll both be there tomorrow. Until then, don't do a thing!" and hung up. The old man put the phone aside and turned to his wife. "Sorted! They're coming for Christmas - and they're paying their own way."

Where do you find elves? It depends where you left them!

Christine got a watch for Christmas. The next day she showed it to her neighbour who said "That's a pretty watch you've got there! Does it tell you the time?" She laughed and said, "No, this is an old-fashioned watch! You have to look at it!"

Why do kids in the Czech Republic get twice as many Christmas presents? Because Santa Clause made a list and he Czeched it twice.

Because she already has everything else, a man buys his mother-in-law a large plot in an expensive cemetery. On the next Christmas, he buys her nothing, so she phones him, furious. "What are you complaining about?" he fires back. "You still haven't used the present I gave you last year."

Why is it so easy to track Santa on Christmas Eve? Because he always accepts cookies.

What did the bald guy say when he was given a comb for Christmas? Thanks, I'll never part with it.

There is a new priest in the church. For the Christmas sermon, a lot of people see him for the first time. He greets everybody at the door but seems rather shy. He's doesn't say much and avoids eye contact. As he steps up to the altar and begins his sermon, he seems transformed. He gives the best speech anyone has ever heard, he's full of confidence, incredibly expressive and has everyone on the edge of their seats. After his sermon, the priest is extremely shy again and barely says a word to anyone. One man approaches the priest and asks "Why are you so shy? You seemed like a different person when you were giving that speech!" "I know..." the priest says, "but that was just my altar ego."

This Christmas my wife said she'd like nothing more than a new car. So I'm getting her what she wanted most.

What did the police officer yell when he saw a snowman stealing? "Freeze!"

After wasting money this Christmas on a new 4K TV. I have a new year's resolution. It's 3840 x 2160.

How does Frosty the Snowman go to the bathroom? That's snowbody's business.

It was autumn, and the Indians on the remote reservation asked their new Chief if the winter was going to be cold or mild. Since he was an Indian Chief in modern society, he had never been taught the old secrets. When he looked at the sky, he couldn't tell what the weather was going to be. Nevertheless, to be on the safe side, he replied to his tribe that the winter was indeed going to be cold and that the members of the village should collect firewood to be prepared. Also, being a practical leader, after several days he got an idea. He went to the phone booths, called the National Weather Service and asked "Is the coming winter going to be cold?" "It looks like this winter is going to be quite cold indeed", the meteorologist at the weather service responded. So the Chief went back to his people and told them to collect even more wood in order to be prepared. A week later, he called the National Weather Service again. "Is it going to be a cold winter?" "Yes," the man at the National Weater Service again replied, "It's definitely going to be a very cold winter." The Chief again went back to his people and ordered them to collect every scrap of wood they could find. Two weeks later, he called the National Weather Service again. "Are you absolutely sure that the winter is going to be very cold?" "Absolutely," the man replied. "It's going to be one of the coldest winters ever." "How can you be so sure?" the Chief asked. The weatherman replied, "The Indians are collections wood like crazy."

Turns out the abominable snowman is actually quite nice. I asked if he had something hot to drink. He answered "Yea Tea".

Charlie says to his friend Dan: My wife hasn't been feeling very festive lately, but I've gotten her a present that will help her to discover the true meaning of Christmas." "What is it?", Dan asks. "A dictionary."

Why did Yoda turn Santa's sleigh around? Because he always reverses clauses.

What do you call Eggs Benedict served during Christmas? Happy Hollandaise.

An ad in the paper was saying: "If anybody knows of any lonely people who will be eating Christmas dinner alone because they have no family or close friends, can they let me know? I need to borrow some chairs."

What do you call a grasshopper that forgot the words to "We Wish You a Merry Christmas?" A "hum" bug.

What do you call a snowman without a carrot? Nobody nose.

A man visits a Christmas market and spots a man with a tiny pony. He walks up to the man and asks: "What's with the pony?" "For a little bit of money the pony can do any trick you ask of it" the man replies. "That's cool," the guy says, and proceeds to take out his wallet. He retrieves some money and puts it in the jar next to the pony. He extends his hand and says "Shake!" The pony promptly performs the trick. The man puts some more money into the jar. "Play dead!" The pony collapses to the ground, then gets up after a little while. "How about a tougher one?" the man says and pays again. "What's eleven minus five?" The pony stomps six times with his hoove. "This is incredible" the man exclaims. He continues to put more and more money into the jar while the pony performs every trick or task without a fault. After a while the guy runs out of money and turns to the man and says: "Sir, that is one incredible animal you have there, is there anything it can't do?" "He can't sing" the man replies. The man considers this for a bit. "Why can't he sing" he finally asks. The owner looks him in the eye and says "He's a little horse."

A woman talks to her friend about the Christmas present she's giving to her boyfriend. "He asked for a pair of gloves for his football games. They were really expensive, but I wanted to make him happy. You know, he's a keeper."

Why did the snowball cross the road? To get to another size.

How much does it cost to run Santa's sleigh every Christmas? Eight bucks. Nine bucks in bad weather.

Five years ago today I pleaded with my snowman not to attempt the river crossing but he wouldn't listen and is lost to me forever. It's water under the bridge now.

Why are friends like snowflakes? When you pee on them, they disappear.

Can you name all of Santa's reindeer? No, they already have names.

What is the wettest animal at the North Pole? The rain-deer.

Somebody asked me recently why I took up downhill skiing. I told them uphill skiing was far too difficult.

Why is dating a snowman so tough? Because his parents will never warm up to you.

A couple is going out for a Christmas party, but as they reach the door, the husband remembers that he forgot to let the cat out. So he runs back into the house while his wife already gets into the taxi. She doesn't want to let the driver know that the house will be empty all night, so she says, "My husband just went to say goodnight to my mother." After a few minutes, the husband comes back and gets into the cab, saying, "Sorry, the thing was hiding under the bed, and I had to poke it with a coat hanger to get it to come out!"

Mitchell decided to spend his Christmas in a ski resort. Before his first trip down the mountain, he heard an unbelievable rumble, and before he could move, he was covered in snow. He found shelter in a small cave and was able to start a fire and make himself comfortable until help arrived. After a few hours, there was a digging at the front of the cave. "Who's there?" Mitchell called out from inside the cave. "Hello!" a voice called. "It's the Red Cross!" "Beat it!" Mitchell yelled back. "I already donated twice this year."

Why did Mickey Mouse get hit with a snowball? Because Donald ducked.

What's one snowball plus one snowball plus one snowball? A Snowman.

What will happen when the Earth's magnetic poles flip? I don't know, but I heard Santa's been interviewing penguins to see if they can pull a sleigh.

Why do birds fly to warmer climates in the winter? Because it is easier than walking!

A man wants to give his wife perfume for Christmas. So he walks into a perfumery and asks for the most exquisite fragrance. "Doobie woobie boop bop", says the assistant. Confused the man looks around and notices that all of the bottles on the shelves are empty. "Do you keep them in the back?" he asks. "Tim tam tibidy tam", says the assistant. The man sniffs the air, then looks at him strangely and asks, "come to think of it, I can't smell a single thing in here, do you even make perfume?" "Flibbidy doo wop, bing bong flam", says the assistant. Confused, the man leaves the store and on his way out bumps into another customer and says, "Don't bother, he doesn't make any scents".

How can you make a Christmas tree happy? Take off the candles, it'll be delighted.

Did you know that a cyclops' favorite winter activity is skiing? It's like skiing, but with one "eye".

How does Santa Claus remember which chimneys he's been down? He keeps a log.

Macy went on a date with a guy and is telling her friend about it. "I don't think I'll see him again, he was a lot like a chocolate Santa Claus. On the outside sweet but hollow and disappointing on the inside."

What do breads do at Christmas dinner? They toast.

An English couple decided to adopt a little German boy. After two years, the child doesn't speak and his parents start to worry about him. After three years, he still has not spoken and after four years, he has yet to utter a word. The English couple figure he is never going to speak but he is still a lovely child, and on the next Christmas eve, they get him a lot of presents and make him his favourite chocolate cake as a dessert. As a special treat, the mother writes "Merry Christmas" with green icing on top of it. The parents are in the kitchen when the boy comes in and says, "Mother, Father, I do not care for the green icing on the chocolate cake." "My God," says his mother. "You can speak?" To which the German boy replies, "Of course." "How come you've never spoken before?" asks his father. "Well," says the boy, "up until now, everything has been satisfactory."

A man was walking down the street when a very dirty and shabby-looking homeless man approached him to ask for a bit of money. It is Christmas, so the man decided to show some sympathy. He took out his wallet, but then stopped. "If I give you this money, will you buy some beer with it instead of dinner?" "No, I stopped drinking years ago," the homeless man replied. "Will you use it to meet with your friends and play cards?" the man asked. "No, I don't waste time playing cards," the homeless man said. "I need to spend all my time trying to stay alive." "Will you watch football instead of buying food with this?" he asked. "I haven't seen a football match in 20 years!", replied the homeless man. "Well," the man said, "I'm not going to give you money. Instead, I'm going to take you home for a shower and a terrific Christmas dinner cooked by my wife." The homeless man was astounded. "Won't your wife be furious with you for doing that?" The other man replied, "Don't worry about that. It's important for her to see what a man looks like after he has given up drinking, playing cards and football."

Patricia is telling her friends about how she spent the Christmas holidays: "It was fun until we went on the skiing trip. It was all downhill from there."

What do you call a snowman with a six pack? An abdominal snowman.

A little boy was standing at the bus stop eating a giant chocolate Santa Claus. A man that was passing by said "Hey kid, eating that much chocolate at one time is bad for you." The little boy looked the man in the eye and said, "Well, my grandpa lived to 103." "Oh, really? Did he eat a lot of chocolate?" "No, heminded his own business."

How did the hipster burn his mouth from hot chocolate? He drank it before it was cool.

A woman is preparing a French dinner for Christmas and sends her husband out to buy some fresh snails. The husband buys the snails then goes into the pub for a quick drink. One thing leads to another and he stays for a few rounds, so many in fact, that by the time he leaves it's nine in the evening. Realizing he's extremely late the husband runs home, pours the snails over the path leading to his house, then he rings the bell. His furious wife opens the door. "Where the hell have you been?" she screams. The husband waves back to the snails, 'Come on, lads!' he shouts "We're nearly there!"

I'm so disappointed. I bought dessert for a traditional German Christmas dinner. But it was stollen.

A man decides to stay in a monastery over Christmas. Everything is lovely. He feels like he is finally finding himself again. The monks tend to be rather silent. Then, at dinner, one of them stands up and says, "16". The other monks all laugh heartily and then go back to eating their meal in silence. A few minutes later another monk stands up and says "32", at which point all the monks collapse into gales of laughter. The Abbott laughs so much that tears run down his cheeks. When everyone is eating again the visitor says to the Abbott, "I don't understand, father. Why do you all laugh when someone says a number?" "Well," says the Abbott, "we all love jokes. But we are a closed community, and so all the jokes are well-known by everyone. To save time, we wrote the jokes down and gave each of them a number. So if one of us says a number we all remember the relevant joke "Could I have a go?" asks the visitor and the Abbott says that will be fine. So, a few minutes later the visitor stands up and says "24". But this time no-one laughs. All the monks look at him in silence and then go back to their meal. "I don't understand it. Why did no-one laugh when I said '24'?" asks the visitor. "I don't know," says the Abbott. Maybe it's the way you tell 'em."

How did Mary and Joseph know that Jesus was 7lbs 2oz? They had a weigh in a manger.

Why can't penguins play football? Because there's snowball.

What does a blind man use to ski? A skiing eye dog.

A woman and her daughter are hosting a Christmas dinner party for some friends. When all the guests arrive, the woman asks the little girl to say grace. She says, "But Mommy, I don't know what to say?" The mother says, "You've heard me pray. Just say what you've heard me say." So the girl says, "Jesus, what was I thinking inviting all these people over to my house?"

I just burned 2000 calories after my Christmas feast. That's the last time I leave brownies in the oven while I nap.

After Christmas, a woman finds her husband rummaging through the fridge, ravenously devouring leftovers from their Thanksgiving feast. "Honey can you stop eating like that? You aren't even heating your food!" she says. To which the husband replies, "Everyone knows it is futile to try and quit cold turkey!"

Don't ever attend Christmas with a group of comedians.They'll never stop roasting the turkey.

Angela tells her friends: "I wanted to make a nice herby chicken dish for Christmas dinner but scratched my plans. I didn't have the thyme for it."

Clark says to Darryl: "I didn't believe my wife when she said she could make a delicious Christmas dinner out of an electric eel. But when I tried it, I was shocked!"

I'm told I'm not very good at cooking, I made a rhubarb Christmas pie, 3 feet long and 2 inches wide!

I'll never forget the Christmas Eve my father went to jail. It didn't take long before he got angry, started yelling and throwing thing. I'll never play Monopoly with him again.

What did the turmeric say when there was a knock on the door during Christmas Dinner? "Cumin! Tis' the season!"

Be extra careful on the roads with the holidays around the corner. A lot of men will be drinking and getting their wives to drive.

Why don't ants catch colds? They have tiny anty bodies.

What did the log say to the Christmas tree? Stay away from lumberjacks or yule end up like me.

After having spent hours in the kitchen to prepare a Christmas dinner, Josephine watches anxiously as her husband's parents eat. Finally, she turns to her mother in law. "How did you find the turkey?" Her mother in law smiles "It was easy, it was right next to the potatoes!"

A man got a new expensive watch for Christmas and proudly wore it to a New Years party, but after being there for about two hours, he found that his watch had been stolen. He searched the party for hours trying to find it, but to no avail. He was getting more and more upset. As the party started to wind down, he began to lose hope of ever finding. Until he saw a drunk man harassing a girl, he was grabbing her arm, trying to get her to come with him. All the while he was standing on the other man's watch "Stop you're hurting me", the girl cried. The man ran over there and punched the drunk straight in the nose. As the girl was still sniffling, she said: "Thank you for saving me." His only reply was "No problem ma'am, no one, and I mean no one treats a lady like that. Not on my watch."

It's really cold outside today, but don't worry, this is an inside joke.

For Christmas, the only gift I got my wife is an alarm clock that swears at her instead of beeping. She's in for a rude awakening.

Every year for Christmas my mom spends a fortune on sending me a gourmet selection of high-quality cashews, pistachios and almonds. Specially selected and seasoned, I googled how much she's been spending on these gifts: around $1,000. It's just nuts.

What's the perfect gift for a weightlifter? A T-shirt, and don't worry about the size. If it's too large they'll be flattered, if it's too small they'll wear it.

What part of a contract entitles you to free gifts? The Santa Clause.

My caribou pal just got me the most thoughtful gift for Christmas. He's always been a deer.

What should a snowman never ask a rabbit? Can you scratch my nose?

Angela tells her friend: "This year for Christmas I wanted to try something new. So I decided to try to smoke a fish this weekend." "How did it go?" her friend asks. "Not too good, I just couldn't figure out which end to light!

How do Eskimos make their beds? With sheets of ice and blankets of snow.

Why did the snowman name his dog frost? Because frost bites.

The inn that turned away Joseph and Mary got a horrible Yelp review. Only one star.

Why don't mountains get cold in the winter? They wear snowcaps.

Where does a polarbear keep its money? In a snow bank!

What does Frosty the Snow Man use to go online? The Winternet!

Gale talks to his friend Milton: "I would like to donate some money now that it's Christmas, but given that I'm an atheist I don't know what charity I should pick." Milton thinks for a moment, and then he replies: "How about a Non Prophet Organization?

A wife texts husband on a cold winter's morning: "Windows frozen, won't open." Her husband texts back: "Gently pour some lukewarm water over it and then gently tap edges with hammer." Ten minutes pass, then he receives another text: "Computer really messed up now."

When I was a kid, every Christmas I would look for sooty footprints near our fireplace. I was looking for Santa clues.

What do you call a letter sent up the chimney on Christmas Eve? Black mail!

One of Santa's reindeers walks into a pub and orders a pint of beer. The barman says $18 please. The reindeer pays and takes a seat. Bemused, the barman approaches and says "this is exciting - we don't get many reindeer in here!", to which the reindeer replies: "I'm not surprised with beer at $18 a pint."

What do you call a muscular snowman? Jacked Frost.

What is a polar bear's favourite thing to eat? Burrrr - Gurrrrs.

Why did the Grinch not steal any kitchen utensils? He decided it wasn't worth the whisk.

Did you know that they've started offering free meditation retreats at the North Pole? It turns out the Christmas elves are present-minded.

A woman hoped her husband would help her address the Christmas cards, since she had a lot to do. She arranged everything they would need, then pulled up a chair and said, "Come on, Dear, let's get these out of the way." He glanced at the array on the table, turned away and went into the den, only to return moments later with a high stack of cards, stamped, sealed, and addressed. "They're last year's," he said. "I forgot to mail them. Now let's go out to dinner and relax."

Why is Frosty the snowman so friendly? Because he's an ice guy!

Why is it so hard to be a detective in the North Pole? Everything is a cold case.

How did the two snowmen know they were meant for each other? It was love at frost sight.

Why does Santa Claus always carry that big bag of gifts? That's just how he presents himself.

Why was the turkey in the pop group? Because he was the only one with drumsticks!

What do snowmen wear on their heads? Ice caps.

Why was the snowman looking through the carrots? He was picking his nose.

Two snowmen were standing in a field. One said, "Can you smell carrots?"

What did Adam say the day before Christmas? "It's Christmas Eve"

What does Santa do with fat elves? He sends them to an Elf Farm.

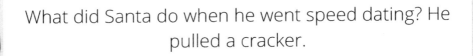

What did Santa do when he went speed dating? He pulled a cracker.

What's a dog's favourite carol? Bark, the herald angels sing.

What do snowmen have for breakfast? Snowflakes

What does Father Christmas do when his elves misbehave? He gives them the sack.

What do you give a dog for Christmas? A mobile bone

Why are Christmas trees very bad at knitting? Because they always drop their needles.

How do snowmen get around? By riding an 'icicle.

What is the best Christmas present? A broken drum, you can't beat it!

Why did Santa have to go to the hospital? Because of his poor elf.

How do you know if Santa's been in your garden shed? You've got three extra hoes.

MERRY
CHRISTMAS

Printed in Great Britain
by Amazon

13760141R00045